Focus

HBR EMOTIONAL INTELLIGENCE SERIES

HBR Emotional Intelligence Series

How to be human at work

The HBR Emotional Intelligence Series features smart, essential reading on the human side of professional life from the pages of *Harvard Business Review*.

Authentic Leadership	*Leadership Presence*
Confidence	*Mindful Listening*
Dealing with Difficult People	*Mindfulness*
Empathy	*Purpose, Meaning, and Passion*
Focus	*Resilience*
Happiness	*Self-Awareness*
Influence and Persuasion	

Other books on emotional intelligence from *Harvard Business Review*:

HBR Everyday Emotional Intelligence

HBR Guide to Emotional Intelligence

HBR's 10 Must Reads on Emotional Intelligence

Focus

HBR EMOTIONAL INTELLIGENCE SERIES

Harvard Business Review Press

Boston, Massachusetts

Library of Congress Cataloging-in-Publication Data

Title: Focus.
Other titles: HBR emotional intelligence series.
Description: Boston, Massachusetts : Harvard Business Review Press, [2018]
   Series: HBR emotional intelligence series
Identifiers: LCCN 2018022310 | ISBN 9781633696587 (pbk. : alk. paper)
Subjects: LCSH: Attention. | Interest (Psychology) | Executives—Psychology. |
   Leadership. | Emotional intelligence.
Classification: LCC BF323.I52 F63 2018 | DDC 658.4/094--dc23
LC record available at https://lccn.loc.gov/2018022310

ISBN: 978-1-63369-658-7
eISBN: 978-1-63369-659-4

Contents

Contents

Contents

Focus

1

The Focused Leader

By Daniel Goleman

A primary task of leadership is to direct attention. To do so, leaders must learn to focus their own attention. When we speak about being focused, we commonly mean thinking about one thing while filtering out distractions. But a wealth of recent research in neuroscience shows that we focus in many ways, for different purposes, drawing on different neural pathways—some of which work in concert, while others tend to stand in opposition.

Grouping these modes of attention into three broad buckets—focusing on *yourself*, focusing on *others*, and focusing on *the wider world*—sheds new light on the practice of many essential leadership skills. Focusing inward and focusing constructively on others helps leaders cultivate the primary elements of emotional intelligence. A fuller understanding of how they focus on the wider world can improve their ability to devise strategy, innovate, and manage organizations.

Every leader needs to cultivate this triad of awareness, in abundance and in the proper balance, because a failure to focus inward leaves you rudderless, a failure to focus on others renders you clueless, and a failure to focus outward may leave you blindsided.

Focusing on yourself

Emotional intelligence begins with self-awareness—getting in touch with your inner voice. Leaders who heed their inner voices can draw on more resources to make better decisions and connect with their authentic selves. But what does that entail? A look at how people focus inward can make this abstract concept more concrete.

Self-awareness

Hearing your inner voice is a matter of paying careful attention to internal physiological signals. These subtle cues are monitored by the insula, which is tucked behind the frontal lobes of the brain. Attention given to any part of the body amps up the insula's sensitivity to that part. Tune in to your heartbeat, and the insula activates more neurons in that circuitry. How well people can sense their heartbeats has, in fact, become a standard way to measure their self-awareness.

Gut feelings are messages from the insula and the amygdala, which neuroscientist Antonio Damasio, of the University of Southern California, calls "somatic markers." Those messages are sensations that something "feels" right or wrong. Somatic markers simplify decision making by guiding our attention toward better options. They're hardly foolproof (how

5

often was that feeling that you left the stove on correct?), so the more comprehensively we read them, the better we use our intuition. (See the sidebar "Are You Skimming This Sidebar?")

Consider, for example, the implications of an analysis of interviews conducted by a group of British researchers with 118 professional traders and 10 senior managers at four City of London investment banks. The most-successful traders (whose annual income averaged £500,000) were neither the ones who relied entirely on analytics nor the ones who just went with their guts. They focused on a full range of emotions, which they used to judge the value of their intuition. When they suffered losses, they acknowledged their anxiety, became more cautious, and took fewer risks. The least-successful traders (whose income averaged only £100,000) tended to ignore their anxiety and keep going with their gut. Because they failed to heed a wider array of internal signals, they were misled.

Zeroing in on sensory impressions of ourselves in the moment is one major element of self-awareness. But another is critical to leadership: combining our experiences across time into a coherent view of our authentic selves.

To be authentic is to be the same person to others as you are to yourself. In part that entails paying attention to what others think of you, particularly people whose opinions you esteem and who will be candid in their feedback. A variety of focus that is useful here is *open awareness,* in which we broadly notice what's going on around us without getting caught up in or swept away by any particular thing. In this mode we don't judge, censor, or tune out; we simply perceive.

Leaders who are more accustomed to giving input than to receiving it may find this tricky. Someone who has trouble sustaining open awareness typically gets snagged by irritating details, such as fellow travelers in the airport security line who take forever getting

ARE YOU SKIMMING THIS SIDEBAR?

Do you have trouble remembering what someone has just told you in conversation? Did you drive to work this morning on autopilot? Do you focus more on your smartphone than on the person you're having lunch with?

Attention is a mental muscle; like any other muscle, it can be strengthened through the right kind of exercise. The fundamental rep for building deliberate attention is simple: When your mind wanders, notice that it has wandered, bring it back to your desired point of focus, and keep it there as long as you can. That basic exercise is at the root of virtually every kind of meditation. Meditation builds concentration and calmness and facilitates recovery from the agitation of stress.

So does a video game called Tenacity, developed by a design group and neuroscientists. The game offers a leisurely journey through any of half a dozen scenes, from a barren desert to a fantasy staircase spiraling heavenward. At the beginner's level you tap an iPad screen with one finger every time you exhale; the challenge is to tap two fingers with every fifth breath. As you move to higher levels, you're presented with more distractions—a helicopter flies into view, a plane does a flip, a flock of birds suddenly scuds by.

When players are attuned to the rhythm of their breathing, they experience the strengthening of selective attention as a feeling of calm focus, as in meditation. Stanford University is exploring that connection at its Calming Technology Lab, which is developing relaxing devices, such as a belt that detects your breathing rate. Should a chock-full inbox, for instance, trigger what has been called "email apnea," an iPhone app can guide you through exercises to calm your breathing and your mind.

their carry-ons into the scanner. Someone who can keep her attention in open mode will notice the travelers but not worry about them, and will take in more of her surroundings. (See the sidebar "Expand Your Awareness.")

Of course, being open to input doesn't guarantee that someone will provide it. Sadly, life affords us few chances to learn how others really see us and even fewer for executives as they rise through the ranks. That may be why one of the most popular and over-enrolled courses at Harvard Business School is Bill George's Authentic Leadership Development, in which George has created what he calls True North groups to heighten this aspect of self-awareness.

These groups (which anyone can form) are based on the precept that self-knowledge begins with self-revelation. Accordingly, they are open and intimate, "a safe place," George explains, "where members can discuss personal issues they do not feel they can raise elsewhere—often not even with their closest family members." What good does that do? "We don't know who we are until we hear ourselves speaking the story of our lives to those we trust," George says. It's a structured way to match our view of our true selves with the views our most trusted colleagues have—an external check on our authenticity.

Self-control

"Cognitive control" is the scientific term for putting one's attention where one wants it and keeping it there in the face of temptation to wander. This focus is one aspect of the brain's executive function, which is located in the prefrontal cortex. A colloquial term for it is "willpower."

Cognitive control enables executives to pursue a goal despite distractions and setbacks. The same neural circuitry that allows such a single-minded pursuit of goals also manages unruly emotions. Good cognitive control can be seen in people who stay calm

EXPAND YOUR AWARENESS

Just as a camera lens can be set narrowly on a single point or more widely to take in a panoramic view, you can focus tightly or expansively.

One measure of open awareness presents people with a stream of letters and numbers, such as S, K, O, E, 4, R, T, 2, H, P. In scanning the stream, many people will notice the first number, 4, but after that their attention blinks. Those firmly in open awareness mode will register the second number as well.

Strengthening the ability to maintain open awareness requires leaders to do something that verges on the unnatural: cultivate at least sometimes a willingness to not be in control, not offer up their own views, not judge others. That's less a matter of deliberate action than of attitude adjustment.

One path to making that adjustment is through the classic power of positive thinking, because pessimism narrows our focus, whereas positive emotions widen our attention and our receptiveness to the new and unexpected. A simple way to shift into positive mode is to ask yourself, "If everything worked out perfectly in my life, what would I be doing in 10 years?" Why is that effective? Because when you're in an upbeat mood, the University of Wisconsin neuroscientist Richard Davidson has found, your brain's left prefrontal area lights up. That area harbors the circuitry that reminds us how great we'll feel when we reach some long-sought goal.

"Talking about positive goals and dreams activates brain centers that open you up to new possibilities," says Richard Boyatzis, a psychologist at Case Western Reserve. "But if you change the conversation to what you should do to fix yourself, it closes you down . . . You need the negative to survive but the positive to thrive."

in a crisis, tame their own agitation, and recover from a debacle or defeat.

Decades' worth of research demonstrates the singular importance of willpower to leadership success. Particularly compelling is a longitudinal study tracking the fates of all 1,037 children born during a single year in the 1970s in the New Zealand city of Dunedin. For several years during childhood the children were given a battery of tests of willpower, including the psychologist Walter Mischel's legendary "marshmallow test"—a choice between eating one marshmallow right away and getting two by waiting 15 minutes. In Mischel's experiments, roughly a third of children grab the marshmallow on the spot, another third hold out for a while longer, and a third manage to make it through the entire quarter hour.

Years later, when the children in the Dunedin study were in their thirties and all but 4% of them had been tracked down again, the researchers found that those who'd had the cognitive control to resist the marshmallow longest were significantly healthier, more successful financially, and more law-abiding than the ones who'd been unable to hold out at all. In fact, statistical analysis showed that a child's level of self-control was a more powerful predictor of financial success than IQ, social class, or family circumstance.

How we focus holds the key to exercising willpower, Mischel says. Three subvarieties of cognitive control are at play when you pit self-restraint against self-gratification: the ability to voluntarily disengage your focus from an object of desire; the ability to resist distraction so that you don't gravitate back to that object; and the ability to concentrate on the future goal and imagine how good you will feel when you achieve it. As adults the children of Dunedin may have been held hostage to their younger selves, but they need not have been, because the power to focus can be developed. (See the sidebar "Learning Self-Restraint.")

LEARNING SELF-RESTRAINT

Quick, now. Here's a test of cognitive control. In what direction is the middle arrow in each row pointing?

$$\rightarrow \rightarrow \rightarrow \leftarrow \leftarrow$$
$$\rightarrow \leftarrow \leftarrow \leftarrow \leftarrow$$
$$\rightarrow \rightarrow \leftarrow \rightarrow \rightarrow$$

The test, called the Eriksen Flanker Task, gauges your susceptibility to distraction. When it's taken under laboratory conditions, differences of a thousandth of a second can be detected in the speed with which subjects perceive which direction the middle arrows are pointing. The stronger their cognitive control, the less susceptible they are to distraction.

Interventions to strengthen cognitive control can be as unsophisticated as a game of Simon Says or Red Light, Green Light—any exercise in which you are asked to stop on cue. Research suggests that the better a child gets at playing Musical Chairs, the stronger his or her prefrontal wiring for cognitive control will become.

Operating on a similarly simple principle is a social and emotional learning (SEL) method that's used to strengthen cognitive control in schoolchildren across the United States. When confronted by an upsetting problem, the children are told to think of a traffic signal. The red light means stop, calm down, and think before you act. The yellow light means slow down and think of several possible solutions. The green light means try out a plan and see how it works. Thinking in these terms allows the children to shift away from amygdala-driven impulses to prefrontal-driven deliberate behavior.

It's never too late for adults to strengthen these circuits as well. Daily sessions of mindfulness practice work in a way similar to Musical Chairs and SEL.

(Continued)

LEARNING SELF-RESTRAINT

In these sessions you focus your attention on your breathing and practice tracking your thoughts and feelings without getting swept away by them. Whenever you notice that your mind has wandered, you simply return it to your breath. It sounds easy—but try it for 10 minutes, and you'll find there's a learning curve.

Focusing on others

The word "attention" comes from the Latin *attendere*, meaning "to reach toward." This is a perfect definition of focus on others, which is the foundation of empathy and of an ability to build social relationships—the second and third pillars of emotional intelligence.

Executives who can effectively focus on others are easy to recognize. They are the ones who find common ground, whose opinions carry the most weight, and with whom other people want to work. They emerge as natural leaders regardless of organizational or social rank.

The empathy triad

We talk about empathy most commonly as a single attribute. But a close look at where leaders are focusing when they exhibit empathy reveals three distinct kinds, each important for leadership effectiveness:

- *Cognitive empathy:* the ability to understand another person's perspective

- *Emotional empathy:* the ability to feel what someone else feels

- *Empathic concern:* the ability to sense what another person needs from you

Cognitive empathy enables leaders to explain themselves in meaningful ways—a skill essential to getting the best performance from their direct reports.

Contrary to what you might expect, exercising cognitive empathy requires leaders to think about feelings rather than to feel them directly.

An inquisitive nature feeds cognitive empathy. As one successful executive with this trait puts it, "I've always just wanted to learn everything, to understand anybody that I was around—why they thought what they did, why they did what they did, what worked for them, and what didn't work." But cognitive empathy is also an outgrowth of self-awareness. The executive circuits that allow us to think about our own thoughts and to monitor the feelings that flow from them let us apply the same reasoning to other people's minds when we choose to direct our attention that way.

Emotional empathy is important for effective mentoring, managing clients, and reading group dynamics. It springs from ancient parts of the brain beneath the cortex—the amygdala, the hypothalamus, the hippocampus, and the orbitofrontal cortex—that allow us to feel fast without thinking deeply. They tune us in by arousing in our bodies the emotional states of others: I literally feel your pain. My brain patterns match up with yours when I listen to you tell a gripping story. As Tania Singer, the director of the social neuroscience department at the Max Planck Institute for Human Cognitive and Brain Sciences in Leipzig, Germany, says, "You need to understand your own feelings to understand the feelings of others." Accessing your capacity for emotional empathy depends on combining two kinds of attention: a deliberate focus on your own echoes of someone else's feelings and an open awareness of that person's face, voice, and other external signs of emotion. (See the sidebar "When Empathy Needs to Be Learned.")

Empathic concern, which is closely related to emotional empathy, enables you to sense not just how people feel but what they need from you. It's what you want in your doctor, your spouse—and your boss. Empathic concern has its roots in the circuitry that

WHEN EMPATHY NEEDS TO BE LEARNED

Emotional empathy can be developed. That's the conclusion suggested by research conducted with physicians by Helen Riess, the director of the Empathy and Relational Science Program at Boston's Massachusetts General Hospital. To help the physicians monitor themselves, she set up a program in which they learned to focus using deep, diaphragmatic breathing and to cultivate a certain detachment—to watch an interaction from the ceiling, as it were, rather than being lost in their own thoughts and feelings. "Suspending your own involvement to observe what's going on gives you a mindful awareness of the interaction without being completely reactive," says Riess. "You can see if your own physiology is charged up or balanced. You can notice what's transpiring in the situation." If a doctor realizes that she's feeling irritated, for instance, that may be a signal that the patient is bothered too.

Those who are utterly at a loss may be able to prime emotional empathy essentially by faking it until they make it, Riess adds. If you act in a caring way—looking people in the eye and paying attention to their expressions, even when you don't particularly want to—you may start to feel more engaged.

compels parents' attention to their children. Watch where people's eyes go when someone brings an adorable baby into a room, and you'll see this mammalian brain center leaping into action.

One neural theory holds that the response is triggered in the amygdala by the brain's radar for sensing danger and in the prefrontal cortex by the release of oxytocin, the chemical for caring. This implies that empathic concern is a double-edged feeling. We intuitively experience the distress of another as our own. But in deciding whether we will meet that person's needs, we deliberately weigh how much we value his or her well-being.

Getting this intuition-deliberation mix right has great implications. Those whose sympathetic feelings become too strong may themselves suffer. In the helping professions, this can lead to compassion fatigue; in executives, it can create distracting feelings of anxiety about people and circumstances that are beyond anyone's control. But those who protect themselves by deadening their feelings may lose touch with empathy. Empathic concern requires us to manage our personal distress without numbing ourselves to the pain of others. (See the sidebar "When Empathy Needs to Be Controlled.")

What's more, some lab research suggests that the appropriate application of empathic concern is critical to making moral judgments. Brain scans have revealed that when volunteers listened to tales of people subjected to physical pain, their own brain centers for experiencing such pain lit up instantly. But if the story was about psychological suffering, the higher brain centers involved in empathic concern and compassion took longer to activate. Some time is needed to grasp the psychological and moral dimensions of a situation. The more distracted we are, the less we can cultivate the subtler forms of empathy and compassion.

WHEN EMPATHY NEEDS TO BE CONTROLLED

Getting a grip on our impulse to empathize with other people's feelings can help us make better decisions when someone's emotional flood threatens to overwhelm us.

Ordinarily, when we see someone pricked with a pin, our brains emit a signal indicating that our own pain centers are echoing that distress. But physicians learn in medical school to block even such automatic responses. Their attentional anesthetic seems to be deployed by the temporal-parietal junction and regions of the prefrontal cortex, a circuit that boosts

Building relationships

People who lack social sensitivity are easy to spot—at least for other people. They are the clueless among us. The CFO who is technically competent but bul-

concentration by tuning out emotions. That's what is happening in your brain when you distance yourself from others in order to stay calm and help them. The same neural network kicks in when we see a problem in an emotionally overheated environment and need to focus on looking for a solution. If you're talking with someone who is upset, this system helps you understand the person's perspective intellectually by shifting from the heart-to-heart of emotional empathy to the head-to-heart of cognitive empathy.

lies some people, freezes out others, and plays favorites—but when you point out what he has just done, shifts the blame, gets angry, or thinks that you're the problem—is not trying to be a jerk; he's utterly unaware of his shortcomings.

Social sensitivity appears to be related to cognitive empathy. Cognitively empathic executives do better at overseas assignments, for instance, presumably because they quickly pick up implicit norms and learn the unique mental models of a new culture. Attention to social context lets us act with skill no matter what the situation, instinctively follow the universal algorithm for etiquette, and behave in ways that put others at ease. (In another age this might have been called good manners.)

Circuitry that converges on the anterior hippocampus reads social context and leads us intuitively to act differently with, say, our college buddies than with our families or our colleagues. In concert with the deliberative prefrontal cortex, it squelches the impulse to do something inappropriate. Accordingly, one brain test for sensitivity to context assesses the function of the hippocampus. The University of Wisconsin neuroscientist Richard Davidson hypothesizes that people who are most alert to social situations exhibit stronger activity and more connections between the hippocampus and the prefrontal cortex than those who just can't seem to get it right.

The same circuits may be at play when we map social networks in a group—a skill that lets us navigate the relationships in those networks well. People who excel at organizational influence can not only sense the flow of personal connections but also name the people whose opinions hold most sway—and so focus on persuading those who will persuade others.

Alarmingly, research suggests that as people rise through the ranks and gain power, their ability to perceive and maintain personal connections tends to suffer a sort of psychic attrition. In studying encounters between people of varying status, Dacher Keltner, a psychologist at Berkeley, has found that higher-ranking individuals consistently focus their gaze less on lower-ranking people and are more likely to interrupt or to monopolize the conversation.

In fact, mapping attention to power in an organization gives a clear indication of hierarchy: The longer it takes Person A to respond to Person B, the more relative power Person A has. Map response times across an entire organization, and you'll get a remarkably accurate chart of social standing. The boss leaves emails unanswered for hours; those lower down respond within minutes. This is so predictable that an algorithm for it—called automated social hierarchy detection—has been developed at Columbia University. Intelligence agencies reportedly are applying the algorithm to suspected terrorist gangs to piece together chains of influence and identify central figures.

But the real point is this: Where we see ourselves on the social ladder sets the default for how much attention we pay. This should be a warning to top executives, who need to respond to fast-moving competitive situations by tapping the full range of ideas and talents within an organization. Without a deliberate shift in attention, their natural inclination may be to ignore smart ideas from the lower ranks.

Focusing on the wider world

Leaders with a strong outward focus are not only good listeners but also good questioners. They are visionaries who can sense the far-flung consequences of local decisions and imagine how the choices they make today will play out in the future. They are open to the surprising ways in which seemingly unrelated data can inform their central interests. Melinda and Bill Gates offered up a cogent example when Melinda remarked on *60 Minutes* that her husband was the kind of person who would read an entire book about fertilizer. Charlie Rose asked, "Why fertilizer?" The connection was obvious to Bill, who is constantly looking for technological advances that can save lives on a massive scale. "A few billion people would have to die if we hadn't come up with fertilizer," he replied.

Focusing on strategy

Any business school course on strategy will give you the two main elements: exploitation of your current advantage and exploration for new ones. Brain scans that were performed on 63 seasoned business decision makers as they pursued or switched between exploitative and exploratory strategies revealed the specific circuits involved. Not surprisingly, exploitation requires concentration on the job at hand, whereas exploration demands open awareness to recognize new possibilities. But exploitation is accompanied by activity in the brain's circuitry for anticipation and reward. In other words, it feels good to coast along in a familiar routine. When we switch to exploration, we have to make a deliberate cognitive effort to disengage from that routine in order to roam widely and pursue fresh paths.

What keeps us from making that effort? Sleep deprivation, drinking, stress, and mental overload all interfere with the executive circuitry used to make the cognitive switch. To sustain the outward focus that leads to innovation, we need some uninterrupted time in which to reflect and refresh our focus.

The wellsprings of innovation

In an era when almost everyone has access to the same information, new value arises from putting ideas together in novel ways and asking smart questions that open up untapped potential. Moments before we have a creative insight, the brain shows a third-of-a-second spike in gamma waves, indicating the synchrony of far-flung brain cells. The more neurons firing in sync, the bigger the spike. Its timing suggests that what's happening is the formation of a new neural network—presumably creating a fresh association.

But it would be making too much of this to see gamma waves as a secret to creativity. A classic model of creativity suggests how the various modes of attention play key roles. First we prepare our minds by gathering a wide variety of pertinent information, and then we alternate between concentrating intently on the problem and letting our minds wander freely. Those activities translate roughly into vigilance, when while immersing ourselves in all kinds of input, we remain alert for anything relevant to the problem at hand; selective attention to the specific creative challenge; and open awareness, in which we allow our minds to associate freely and the solution to emerge spontaneously. (That's why so many fresh ideas come to people in the shower or out for a walk or a run.)

The dubious gift of systems awareness

If people are given a quick view of a photo of lots of dots and asked to guess how many there are, the strong systems thinkers in the group tend to make the best estimates. This skill shows up in those who are good at designing software, assembly lines, matrix organizations, or interventions to save failing ecosystems—it's a very powerful gift indeed. After all, we live within extremely complex systems. But, suggests the Cambridge University psychologist Simon Baron-Cohen (a cousin of actor Sacha's), in a small but significant number of people, a strong systems awareness is coupled with an empathy deficit—a blind spot for what other people are thinking and feeling and for reading social situations. For that reason, although people with a superior systems understanding are organizational assets, they are not necessarily effective leaders.

An executive at one bank explained to me that it has created a separate career ladder for systems analysts so that they can progress in status and salary on the basis of their systems smarts alone. That way, the bank can consult them as needed while recruiting leaders from a different pool—one containing people with emotional intelligence.

Putting it all together

For those who don't want to end up similarly compartmentalized, the message is clear. A focused leader is not the person concentrating on the three most important priorities of the year, or the most brilliant systems thinker, or the one most in tune with the corporate culture. Focused leaders can command the full range of their own attention: They are in touch with their inner feelings, they can control their impulses, they are aware of how others see them, they understand what others need from them, and they can weed out distractions and also allow their minds to roam widely, free of preconceptions.

This is challenging. But if great leadership were a paint-by-numbers exercise, great leaders would be more common. Practically every form of focus can be strengthened. What it takes is not talent so much as diligence—a willingness to exercise the attention circuits of the brain just as we exercise our analytic skills and other systems of the body.

The link between attention and excellence remains hidden most of the time. Yet attention is the basis of the most essential of leadership skills—emotional, organizational, and strategic intelligence. And never has it been under greater assault. The constant onslaught of incoming data leads to sloppy shortcuts—triaging our email by reading only the subject lines, skipping many of our voicemails, skimming memos and reports. Not only do our habits of attention make us less effective, but the sheer volume of all those messages leaves us too little time to reflect on what they really mean. This was foreseen decades ago by the Nobel Prize–winning economist Herbert Simon. Information "consumes the attention of its recipients," he wrote in 1971. "Hence a wealth of information creates a poverty of attention."

My goal here is to place attention center stage so that you can direct it where you need it when you need it. Learn to master your attention, and you will be in command of where you, and your organization, focus.

DANIEL GOLEMAN is codirector of the Consortium for Research on Emotional Intelligence in Organizations at Rutgers University and coauthor of *Primal Leadership: Unleashing the Power of Emotional Intelligence* (Harvard Business Review Press, 2013). His latest book is *Altered Traits: Science Reveals How Meditation Changes Your Mind, Brain, and Body.*

Reprinted from *Harvard Business Review*,
December 2013 (product #R1312B).

2

Break the Cycle of Stress and Distraction by Using Your Emotional Intelligence

By Kandi Wiens

B eing able to focus helps us succeed.[1] Whether it's focusing inward and attuning ourselves to our intuitions and values or outward and navigating the world around us, honing our attention is a valuable asset.

All too often though, our focus and attention get hijacked, leaving us feeling frazzled, forgetful, and unable to concentrate. In my coaching work with executives, these are the kinds of statements I most often hear when they've lost their focus (I may have uttered a few of them myself):

- "I feel completely overwhelmed."

- "My workload is insane, and there's never enough time to get things done when I'm in meetings and dealing with urgent issues all day long."

- "I'm mentally exhausted from the pressure and constant distractions in my office. I just can't seem to focus."

Constant distractions and a lack of time certainly interrupt our focus, but stress also plays a major role.[2]

Chronic stress floods our nervous system with cortisol and adrenaline that short-circuits important cognitive functions.[3] Researchers have studied the negative effects of stress on focus, memory, and other cognitive functions for decades. The findings are consistent: Short-term stress raises cortisol levels (the so-called stress hormone) for short periods and can jump-start our adrenaline and motivate us to perform more efficiently in response to impending deadlines.[4] Long-term stress, however, can lead to prolonged increases in cortisol and can be toxic to the brain. Scientists also suspect that high levels of cortisol over a long period of time are a key contributor to Alzheimer's and other forms of dementia.[5]

When we can't focus at work because of distractions, it may lead us to feel stressed about not being productive, which then causes us to focus less, further feeding the cycle. Unfortunately, most of us don't notice our focus declining until we become completely overwhelmed. When mental and emotional exhaustion sets in, it further drains our ability to focus, concentrate, and recall information.

Fortunately, there are things we can do to break the cycle. I've found in my research that one of the reasons why some people get burned out and others don't is because they use their emotional intelligence (EI) to manage their stress.[6] You can use these same competencies, in particular self-awareness and self-management, to improve your focus. Here's how.

Start by using your self-awareness to help you notice several things:

- *Why you feel stressed or anxious.* Before you can deal with stress, you need to know what's causing it. As simple as it may sound, it can be helpful to make a list of the sources of your stress. Write down each thing in your life and at work that's causing you anxiety. You might categorize items into things you have the ability to change and things you don't. For the stressors in the latter category, you will need to figure out how to change your attitude toward them.[7]

- *How you lose your ability to focus.* According to clinical psychologist Michael Lipson, you can learn to sharpen your focus by understanding how exactly your concentration strays in the first place.[8] By paying attention to the patterns that lead to your lack of focus, you can begin to develop your ability to dismiss distractions and stay with your original point of attention.

- *How you feel when you can't focus.* Does it make you anxious when you can't recall information when you need it—perhaps during a job interview, a high-stakes presentation, or an important client meeting? Do you feel tense and dazed when you're racking your brain trying to find just the right words for an important email? These can be clues that you're more stressed than you may realize—and that your inability to concentrate is causing even more stress.

- *When you lose your ability to focus.* If, for example, you find yourself worrying yourself sick over something while you're driving 65 mph on the highway with a car full of kids, you're putting yourself and others in real danger. This can be a wake-up call to bring your attention back to what you're doing and make a decision to think about your concerns later.

Once you've increased your awareness of what's causing you stress and how and when you lose your focus, you can use the following strategies, which depend on your self-management abilities, to make better choices that keep you focused.

- *Do a digital detox.*[9] In its 2017 Stress in America survey, The American Psychological Association (APA) found that "constant checkers"—people who check their emails, texts, and social media on a constant basis—experience more stress than those who don't.[10] More than 42% of respondents attribute their stress to political and cultural discussions on social media, compared with 33% of non-constant checkers. While it may feel impossible to take a cold turkey break from technology, the APA says that periodically unplugging or limiting your digital access can be great for your mental health.

- *Rest your brain.* Most of us have experienced sleepless nights caused by ruminating over past events or fears and anxieties about the future. When you add a few of these nights together, sleep deprivation can set in, making it more difficult to focus and more challenging to receive and recall information.[11] Our interpretation of events and our judgment may be affected, too.[12] Lack of sleep can negatively affect our decisions because it impairs our ability to accurately assess a situation, plan accordingly, and behave appropriately. Committing to the recommended seven to eight hours of sleep each night may seem impossible when you're stressed and overworked, but the payoff is worth it.[13]

- *Practice mindfulness.* The research on mindfulness is clear and compelling. Having a mindfulness practice decreases our tendency to jump to conclusions and have knee-jerk reactions we may regret later (and potentially cause more stress).[14] Neuroscientist Richard Davidson says that "Mindfulness boosts the classic attention network in the brain's frontoparietal system that works together to allocate attention."[15] In other words, mindfulness is key to emotional resilience, which is a key contributor in our ability to quickly recover from stress. Don't worry, you don't have to be a serious yogi to practice mindfulness.[16]

- *Shift your focus to others.* When we fixate on our own worries and fears, it can take our attention away from those we care about. Studies (mine included) show that shifting our focus to others produces physiological effects that calm us and strengthen our resilience.[17] If you pay more attention to other people's feelings and needs and show concern for them, you can not only take your mind off of your stress but also reap the benefits of knowing that you're doing something meaningful for someone you care about.[18]

Too many people feel like they need to work harder when they struggle to focus. But this strategy is likely to backfire.[19] Instead, pay attention to the causes of your stress and inability to focus, and then take actions that promote improvements in the specific brain functions that drive concentration and awareness.

KANDI WIENS is a faculty member at the University of Pennsylvania Graduate School of Education in the PennCLO executive doctoral program and the Penn Master's in Medical Education program. She is also an executive coach, national speaker, and organizational change consultant.

Notes

1. Daniel Goleman, *Focus: The Hidden Driver of Excellence* (New York: Harper, 2013).
2. William Treseder, "The Two Things Killing Your Ability to Focus," hbr.org, August 3, 2016, https://hbr.org/2016/08/the-two-things-killing-your-ability-to-focus.
3. Madhumita Murgia, "How Stress Affects Your Brain," TED-Ed video, 4:15, https://ed.ted.com/lessons/how-stress-affects-your-brain-madhumita-murgia.
4. Francesca Gino, "Are You Too Stressed to Be Productive? Or Not Stressed Enough?" hbr.org, April 14, 2016, https://

hbr.org/2016/04/are-you-too-stressed-to-be-productive -or-not-stressed-enough.

5. Elaine Karen Hebda-Bauer and Huda Akil, "How Over-expression of a Stress Gene Modifies Alzheimer's Disease Pathology," grant from the Alzheimer's Association, 2007–2010, https://www.alz.org/research/alzheimers_ grants/for_researchers/overview-2007.asp?grants=2007 hebda-bauer.

6. Kandi Weins, "Leading Through Burnout: The Influence of Emotional Intelligence on the Ability of Executive Level Physician Leaders to Cope with Occupational Stress and Burnout," dissertation, University of Pennsylvania, 2016, https://repository.upenn.edu/dissertations/ AAI10158565/.

7. David Brendel, "Stress Isn't a Threat, It's a Signal to Change," hbr.org, May 5, 2014, https://hbr.org/2014/05/ stress-isnt-a-threat-its-a-signal-to-change.

8. Michael Lipson, "To Improve Your Focus, Notice How You Lose It," hbr.org, November 4, 2015, https://hbr.org/2015/ 11/to-improve-your-focus-notice-how-you-lose-it. (This article is reproduced in chapter 3 of this book.)

9. Charlotte Lieberman, "Device-Free Time Is as Important as Work-Life Balance," hbr.org, April 13, 2017, https://hbr .org/2017/04/device-free-time-is-as-important-as-work -life-balance.

10. American Psychological Association, "APA's Survey Finds Constantly Checking Electronic Devices Linked to Significant Stress for Most Americans," press release, Febru-

ary 23, 2017, http://www.apa.org/news/press/releases/
2017/02/checking-devices.aspx.

11. Nick van Dam and Els van der Helm, "There's a Proven
    Link Between Effective Leadership and Getting
    Enough Sleep," hbr.org, February 16, 2016, https://hbr
    .org/2016/02/theres-a-proven-link-between-effective
    -leadership-and-getting-enough-sleep.

12. Cristiano Guarana and Christopher M. Barnes, "Research:
    Sleep Deprivation Can Make It Harder to Stay Calm at
    Work," hbr.org, August 21, 2017, https://hbr.org/2017/08/
    research-sleep-deprivation-can-make-it-harder-to-stay
    -calm-at-work.

13. Larry Rosen, "Relax, Turn Off Your Phone, and Go to
    Sleep," hbr.org, August 31, 2015, https://hbr.org/2017/08/
    research-sleep-deprivation-can-make-it-harder-to-stay
    -calm-at-work.

14. Rasmus Hougaard, Jacqueline Carter, and Gitte Dybkjaer,
    "Spending 10 Minutes a Day on Mindfulness Subtly
    Changes the Way You React to Everything," hbr.org,
    January 18, 2017, https://hbr.org/2017/01/spending-10
    -minutes-a-day-on-mindfulness-subtly-changes-the-way
    -you-react-to-everything

15. Richard J. Davidson and Jon Kabat-Zinn, "Alterations in
    Brain and Immune Function Produced by Mindfulness
    Meditation: Three Caveats: Response," *Psychosomatic
    Medicine* 66, no. 1 (January–February 2004): 149–152.

16. Positive Psychology Program, "22 Mindfulness Exercises,
    Techniques, and Activities for Adults," January 18, 2017,

https://positivepsychologyprogram.com/mindfulness
-exercises-techniques-activities/.

17. Annie McKee and Kandi Wiens, "Prevent Burnout by
Making Compassion a Habit," hbr.org, May 11, 2017,
https://hbr.org/2017/05/prevent-burnout-by-making
-compassion-a-habit.

18. Cassie Mogilner, "You'll Feel Less Rushed If You Give
Time Away," hbr.org, September 2012, https://hbr
.org/2012/09/youll-feel-less-rushed-if-you-give-time
-away.

19. Sarah Green Carmichael, "The Research Is Clear: Long
Hours Backfire for People and for Companies," hbr.org,
August 19, 2015, https://hbr.org/2015/08/the-research-is
-clear-long-hours-backfire-for-people-and-for-companies.

Reprinted from hbr.org, originally published
December 12, 2017 (product #H04351).

3

To Improve Your Focus, Notice How You Lose It

By Michael Lipson

We've all been there: You try to focus on a task, and soon you're looking out the window, wondering about dinner, analyzing your golf game, fantasizing about your lover. How did your mind end up in Cancún when you were supposed to be thinking about first-quarter strategy?

The normal act of concentration or attention is a mess, but it's a mess with a specific structure. To learn to sharpen your focus, you can start by understanding this "structure of distraction"—how, exactly, your concentration strays in the first place.

Over the past 20 years working as a clinical psychologist, I have led workshops and meditation groups that have taught people from all walks of life to see the structure of their own distraction. In my work with clinicians in end-of-life care, understanding this structure has helped them distinguish between the needs of dying patients and their own emotional responses. This same skill has helped families to drop resentments and choose togetherness. It has helped business leaders clarify their strategic goals and develop the courage both to initiate and to end internal and external relationships. It has even helped golf players keep their mind on their swing and their eye on the ball.

What follows is my reformulation of wisdom that has been around since people first noticed they had minds—and simultaneously noticed that the mind could be distracted from its intentional focus. It didn't start with the cell phone, as scholar and innovator Cathy Davidson points out.[1] In Greek mythology, Hercules distracts Atlas and tricks him into losing his focus and his freedom. Homer has Circe distract Odysseus from his journey—probably not the first or last sexual distraction. Plato's Socrates explains in his last dialogue that the mind is normally in shreds, and the purpose of philosophy is to "gather" and concentrate the mind in spite of its centrifugal forces. Shakespeare points to a distracted mind, for example, in Claudius's monologue in *Hamlet*.

Like Plato, most writers not only complain about distraction but point implicitly or explicitly to ways to address its downsides. In the meditative traditions, everyone from Gautama Buddha to mindfulness expert Andy Puddicombe of Headspace has said that the prime way to deal with distraction is first to be okay with it, which means noticing it.[2] You notice the distraction, and bring your mind back.

The approach I use summarizes and condenses the wisdom from these disparate traditions. You begin by simply noticing that there are four phases of attention and distraction that happen every time you try to focus:

1. *First, you choose a focus.* It might be anything, from any sphere of life. At work, it's supposed to be some aspect of work—let's say, whom to include in an important meeting.

2. *Sooner or later, your attention wanders.* This isn't what you plan to do. It just happens. (If it *were* a plan, it would be another focus, not a wandering.)

3. *Sooner or later, you wake up to the fact that your mind has wandered.* You notice the distraction. You realize how far you are from the thing you first wanted to focus on. Again, you can't exactly plan or choose this.

4. *Having woken up, you may choose to return to the original theme.* For example, whom to invite to that meeting. Then again, you may choose to give up and do something else. It's up to you; it's a choice.

If you do return to the original theme at step 4, the whole thing tends to begin again. Sooner or later, your mind wanders.

Reviewing these four steps, you'll notice that steps 1 and 4 are conscious choices. Steps 2 and 3 are unconscious—they just happen. The unconscious force at work in the second step, when your mind "just wanders," seems to be hostile to the project of focusing; the force operating in the third step, when you notice your distraction, is not exactly friendly to your focus, but it is friendly to your freedom. It wakes you up to the fact of having wandered from your theme, then leaves it up to you to return to that original focus or not.

Just by noticing these stages over and over as they play out in real time, you'll find that the pattern changes. At first you may simply note that these four stages occur. With repeated attention to the process, you will tend to stay with the original focus longer before distraction sets in. You will wander less far away from the theme, and for a shorter length of time, before waking up. And having woken up from a distraction, you will choose more often to return to the original theme rather than give up and stretch your legs.

Here's how to get started. Pick a theme, any theme: something you want to focus on that would potentially help your business. It could be a personnel decision, it could be a strategic decision, it could be a management issue. That's step 1, your focus. Think about it as clearly and creatively as you can. Soon, your attention will wander. But the very act of noticing the distraction, and the *structure* of distraction, will gradually strengthen your ability to stay focused and head off distraction in the first place.

MICHAEL LIPSON is a clinical psychologist and a former associate clinical professor at Columbia University's medical school. He is the author of *Stairway of Surprise: Six Steps to a Creative Life*.

Notes

1. Cathy N. Davidson, "The History of Distraction, 4000 BCE to the Present," blog post, November 13, 2011, http://www .cathydavidson.com/blog/the-history-of-distraction-4000 -bce-to-the-present/.
2. Andy Puddicombe, "Headspace," website, 2018, https:// www.headspace.com.

Reprinted from hbr.org, originally published
November 4, 2015 (product #H02GHT).

4

What to Do When You're Feeling Distracted at Work

By Amy Gallo

Sometimes there's so much going on in your life, and in the world, that you can't focus. What can you do when every time you sit down at your desk, you feel distracted? How can you get back to feeling focused and productive?

What the experts say

Feeling distracted and unproductive is something most people struggle with, says Susan David, founder of the Harvard/McLean Institute of Coaching and author of *Emotional Agility*.[1] This is especially true because most of us are constantly bombarded by news alerts, text messages, and other interruptions. And even on days when you might feel industrious, you have to contend with what's going on with your coworkers. "We very subtly pick up on others' behaviors and emotions," David says.[2] "When this happens, we can start to lose our way." Rich Fernandez, CEO of the nonprofit Search Inside Yourself Leadership Institute, a global mindfulness and emotional intelligence training organization, notes that we're actually wired this way. "One thing we all have in common is a fundamental neuroanatomy that orients us toward stress that isn't always productive," he explains. To overcome this and regain your focus, take the following eight steps.

Understand the dangers of multitasking

Start by understanding the impact that distractions, like a constantly pinging phone or quick Twitter break, have on your brain. Fernandez explains that we have a network of brain structures related to focus.[3] There's the *default mode network*, which is responsible for analyzing the past, forecasting or planning for the future, and reflecting on oneself and others. "We're in this mode at least half of the time," he says. But when you need to focus your mind, you tap into the *direct attention network*, which allows you to put aside ruminations and stay on task. Distractions, in whatever form they take, pull you back into default mode, and the cognitive cost of regaining your focus is high.[4] "Some research shows it can take ten to eighteen minutes to get the same level of attention back," Fernandez says.[5] This is why it's critical to reduce interruptions.

Allow for your emotional response, but stay in charge

Feeling overwhelmed can bring up a lot of emotions—frustration, anger, anxiety—that take a further toll on your productivity. So you have to break the cycle,

David says. To regain a sense of agency, so you don't feel "at the mercy of the events going on in the world or in your office," she suggests labeling your feelings and then asking yourself questions about them.[6] You might say, "OK, I'm feeling angry, but who's in charge—the anger or me, the person having the emotion?" Fernandez agrees with this approach: "You want to acknowledge that these feelings are there—they're legitimate and significant—but not get swept away by them."

Gather your attention

When you do find yourself distracted, Fernandez says, "Pause, take stock, be aware that you're being triggered. Then switch the spotlight of your attention." This might feel easier said than done, but remind yourself that most of the things we worry about "aren't immediate existential threats." To reconnect with the logical part of your brain, focus it on "something more immediate or visceral, like your breath." You might say to yourself, "I've become consumed by this Twitter thread. I'm going to pay attention to my breathing" to pivot away from what's causing the anxiety.[7] Fernandez says this isn't the same as trying to ignore the distraction: "You don't have to stifle it or suppress it. Make note of it, acknowledge it, and put it in a mental parking lot to think about later, when you can discuss it with someone else, or when you're not at work and have lots to do."

Rely on your values

Once you've gathered your attention, you can choose where to focus it. David says that concentrating on your values gives you a sense of control. "When you're overwhelmed, it feels like a lot of power and choices are being taken away from you," she says. "But you still get to choose who you want to be. If one of your core values is to be collaborative, focus on that. How can you help people feel like part of the team?" And consider how your lack of focus is affecting your sense of self. "If fairness is important to you, how is your distraction contributing to your ability to be fair? If you're on Facebook for three hours a day, how fair is that to your team or your family?"

Put up boundaries

Once you have more awareness about what distracts you, set rules for yourself. If you realize that checking news in the morning means that you're upset and unfocused when you get to the office, tell yourself that you won't catch up on world events until lunchtime.[8] Or you can decide that you're going to get a certain amount of work done before you go on Facebook. If you don't have the self-control for this, there are apps you can install in your browsers or on your phone to control how much time you spend on particular sites. You also have to practice. "There's a lot of research that suggests the difference between elite focus and non-elite focus is deliberate focus," Fernandez says.[9] He points to athletes who train by telling themselves, for example, "I'm not going to leave the free-throw line until I make 10 free throws." So spend time training your brain to stay on task.

Choose whom you interact with wisely

Social contagion is real. "We've all had that experience when you go into an elevator and everyone is looking at their cell phones, so you start looking at yours," David says. She points to recent research that shows that if someone next to you on an airplane buys candy—even if you don't know the person—you're 30% more likely to make a similar purchase.[10] The same goes for productivity.[11] If you have colleagues who are constantly distracted themselves or who tend to pull you away from work, try to spend less time with them. You don't have to be rude; you can say something simple like, "Can we continue this conversation later? I want to get this report done and then I can take a break."

Support and be supported by your colleagues

Instead of avoiding your distracted colleagues, you could try to encourage each other to stay focused. Make a pact with your coworkers. Set up a time where you will work without interrupting each other or without getting on social media or workplace messaging app Slack. The team I work with at HBR designated Thursday afternoons as uninterrupted work time after listening to a podcast about this.[12] You can take this collegial support one step further and actively support each other. "Your peers are in the trenches with you and they can relate because they're in the same culture and organization," Fernandez says. Go out to coffee with a coworker and "ask for advice, counsel, and coaching." They may have tactics that have worked for them that you haven't thought of. Make a commitment to each other that you're going to change your behavior and check in regularly on your progress. When you tell someone else that you want to reform your ways, you're more likely to follow through.[13]

Take care of your body

If you're tired and worn out, you're going to be more vulnerable to feeling overwhelmed, David says. It's important to get enough sleep and exercise. Also, she suggests making "tiny tweaks in your environment" that improve your well-being.[14] Take breaks, eat a healthy lunch, put your phone on silent. "If you normally spend your lunch hour on Facebook, leave your phone behind and go outside for a walk instead," she says.

Principles to remember

Do:

- Use breathing to break the immediate cycle of anxiety and frustration with being distracted.

- Think about how you want to act as a colleague and a leader, and let that self-image guide your behavior.

- Set boundaries around when you'll go on social media or check email.

Don't:

- Fool yourself into thinking distractions aren't harmful to your focus—they have high cognitive costs.

- Spend time with people who are distracted. You're likely to end up feeling the same way.

- Neglect self-care. Instead, take breaks, eat healthily, and get enough sleep.

Case study #1: Schedule time to focus

Over the past year, Emily Lin, a vice president at a financial services company, had a lot on her plate. She was building her private coaching practice and had received a promotion at work. Because of the expanded scope of her responsibilities, she was dealing with a whole host of new distractions. "I got so many more emails, instant messages, and phone calls. And people were coming by my office much more frequently," she says.

Emily was having trouble getting her work done. "I would see all these instant messages or email alerts popping up, and even if it just took a few seconds to read them or send a quick response, it would take me away from what I was doing," she says. And it was affecting her mood. "Certain messages would stress me out. I was becoming very short-tempered with my coworkers."

She had previously learned to set boundaries for herself around social media by scheduling in time for distractions. "I gave myself pockets of time when I could go on Facebook. It might be a 10-minute break between meetings or while I was waiting for the elevator to go to lunch. Once I baked those breaks in, I found it a lot easier to control the impulse to check social media while I was working," she explains.

She did something similar to address the work interruptions: she allowed herself time to read and respond to messages, but only after getting her most important work completed. "At the beginning of each week, I ask myself, 'What are the most critical things I have to complete?' And each day, I ask, 'Today, what is the one thing I absolutely have to do?'" She says that helped her determine how much time she needed to focus, and then she would block that time out in two-hour chunks. "For a two-hour window, I turn off email, put 'do not disturb' on instant messenger, and send my phone directly to voicemail." She would even put on headphones as a way to signal to would-be visitors that she was busy.

Two hours seems to be the right amount of time, she says. It gives her enough time to get deeply involved in a task, and it's a "tolerable amount of time to be unreachable," she says. "After that, people start to call back or email again." Plus, it gives her a sense of urgency. "I have the adrenaline to get things done."

Emily says this approach has worked: "It's had a noticeable effect on my productivity." And she feels less stressed. "Because I'm not constantly looking at my email throughout the day, my blood pressure isn't always escalated. I'm a lot more patient now when I am interrupted."

She points out that getting more sleep has also helped her resist distractions. A few years ago she was only sleeping three or four hours a night, but she has drastically revamped her sleep schedule and is now getting from six and a half to seven hours a night. "I went from feeling overwhelmed and unable to focus to being able to think clearly," she says. "When I'm well rested, I have more perspective. I know I don't have to respond to an email right away." She's even become "a huge sleep evangelist" with her coaching clients.

Case study #2: Set boundaries

Sarah Taylor (not her real name), an HR manager at an international humanitarian organization, struggled to stay focused at work for several months before and after the 2016 U.S. presidential election. She says she couldn't stay away from the news. "I was spending several hours a day—throughout the workday, not just in the evenings—compulsively checking for updates on various sites, like the *New York Times*, the *Washington Post*, and CNN." Because of these distractions, she would get behind and found herself working late into the evening and on weekends to try to keep up.

"I was miserable because I wasn't getting sufficient rest—not to mention I was being continually exposed to bad news every day." While she knew this wasn't good for her, she struggled to set limits on her own.

She saw a reference to StayFocusd, a browser extension that sets time limits for selected websites. She checked online reviews and saw that it had helped others like her, so she decided to try it out. "At that point, I was desperate to find ways to fix my bad habit, which I was clearly unable to do through my own willpower," she says.

She put a 10-minute daily limit on the three news sites she mentioned earlier. Once that limit has passed, a window pops up that says, "Shouldn't you be working?" She says it definitely helps—though she does find ways around it. "My sneaky mind starts looking at sites that I haven't yet blocked, such as the BBC."

She's set other rules for herself as well. When she works from home, she keeps all of her personal devices out of the room where she's working. She still stays up-to-date on current events, she says, "but at least I'm no longer risking being seriously behind on my core work duties."

AMY GALLO is a contributing editor at *Harvard Business Review* and the author of the *HBR Guide to Dealing with Conflict*. She writes and speaks about workplace dynamics. Follow her on Twitter @amyegallo.

Notes

1. Susan David, *Emotional Agility: Get Unstuck, Embrace Change, and Thrive in Work and Life* (New York: Avery, 2016).
2. Shawn Achor and Michelle Gielan, "Make Yourself Immune to Secondhand Stress," hbr.org, September 2, 2015, https://hbr.org/2015/09/make-yourself-immune-to-secondhand-stress.

3. Matthew McKinnon, "Neuroscience of Mindfulness: Default Mode Network, Meditation, and Mindfulness," mindfulnessmd.com, June 17, 2017, https://www.mindful nessmd.com/2014/07/08/neuroscience-of-mindfulness -default-mode-network-meditation-mindfulness/.

4. Bob Sullivan and Hugh Thompson, "Brain, Interrupted," *New York Times*, May 3, 2013.

5. American Psychological Association, "Multitasking: Switching Costs," March 20, 2006, http://www.apa.org/ research/action/multitask.aspx.

6. Susan David, "3 Ways to Better Understand Your Emotions," hbr.org, November 10, 2016, https://hbr.org/ 2016/11/3-ways-to-better-understand-your-emotions.

7. Leah Weiss, "A Simple Way to Stay Grounded in Stressful Moments," hbr.org, November 18, 2016, https://hbr .org/2016/11/a-simple-way-to-stay-grounded-in-stressful -moments.

8. Shawn Achor and Michelle Gielan, "Consuming Negative News Can Make You Less Effective at Work," hbr.org, September 14, 2015, https://hbr.org/2015/09/consuming -negative-news-can-make-you-less-effective-at-work.

9. K. Anders Ericcson, Michael J. Prietula, and Edward T. Cokely, "The Making of an Expert," *Harvard Business Review*, July–August 2007, 114.

10. Eilene Zimmerman, "Pedro M. Gardete: Fellow Airline Passengers Influence What You Buy," *Insights by Stanford Business*, Stanford Graduate School of Business, February 6, 2015, https://www.gsb.stanford.edu/insights/pedro

-m-gardete-fellow-airline-passengers-influence-what
-you-buy.

11. Jason Corsello and Dylan Minor, "Want to Be More
Productive? Sit Next to Someone Who Is," hbr.org, February 14, 2017, https://hbr.org/2017/02/want-to-be-more
-productive-sit-next-to-someone-who-is.

12. Jason Fried, "Restoring Sanity to the Office," interview
by Sarah Green-Carmichael, *Harvard Business Review*,
Audio, 31:32, December 29, 2016, https://hbr.org/
ideacast/2016/12/restoring-sanity-to-the-office.

13. Rebecca Knight, "Make Your Work Resolutions Stick,"
hbr.org, December 29, 2014, https://hbr.org/2014/12/
make-your-work-resolutions-stick.

14. Amy Jen Su, "6 Ways to Weave Self-Care into Your Workday," hbr.org, June 19, 2017, https://hbr.org/2017/06/6
-ways-to-weave-self-care-into-your-workday.

Reprinted from hbr.org, originally published
December 20, 2017 (product #H0433F).

5

How to Make Yourself Work When You Just Don't Want To

By Heidi Grant

There's that project you've left on the back burner—the one with the deadline that's growing uncomfortably near. And there's the client whose phone call you really should return—the one who does nothing but complain and eat up your valuable time. Wait, weren't you going to try to go to the gym more often this year?

Can you imagine how much less guilt, stress, and frustration you would feel if you could somehow just make yourself do the things you don't want to do when you are actually supposed to do them? Not to mention how much happier and more effective you would be?

The good news (and it's very good news) is that you can get better about not putting things off if you use the right strategy. Figuring out which strategy to use depends on why you are procrastinating in the first place. Here are some of the most likely reasons.

Reason #1: You are putting something off because you are afraid you'll screw it up

Solution: Adopt a "prevention focus"

There are two ways to look at any task. You can do something because you see it as a way to end up better off than you are now—as an achievement or accomplishment. As in, "If I complete this project successfully I will impress my boss," or "If I work out regularly, I will look amazing." Psychologists call this a **promotion focus,** and research shows that when you have one, you are motivated by the thought of making gains, and you work best when you feel eager and optimistic. Sounds good, doesn't it? Well, if you are afraid you will screw up on the task in question, this is *not* the focus type for you. Anxiety and doubt undermine promotion motivation, leaving you less likely to take any action at all.

What you need is a way of looking at what you need to do that *isn't* undermined by doubt but rather, ideally, thrives on it. When you have a **prevention focus**, instead of thinking about how you can end up better off, you see the task as a way to hang on to what you already have—to avoid loss. For the prevention focused, successfully completing a project is a way to keep your boss from being angry or thinking less of you. Working out regularly is a way to not "let yourself go." Decades of research, which I describe in my book *Focus*, shows that prevention motivation is actually enhanced by anxiety about what might go wrong. When you are focused on avoiding loss, it becomes clear that the only way to get out of danger is to take immediate action. The more worried you are, the faster you are out of the gate.

I know this doesn't sound like a barrel of laughs, particularly if you are usually more the promotion-minded type, but there is probably no better way to get over your anxiety about screwing up than to give some serious thought to all the dire consequences of doing nothing at all. So go on, scare the pants off yourself. It feels awful, but it works.

Reason #2: You are putting something off because you don't feel like doing it

Solution: Make like Spock and ignore your feelings. They're getting in your way

In his excellent book *The Antidote: Happiness for People Who Can't Stand Positive Thinking*, Oliver

Burkeman points out that often when we say things like "I just can't get out of bed early in the morning," or "I just can't get myself to exercise," what we really mean is that we can't get ourselves to *feel* like doing these things. After all, no one is tying you to your bed every morning. Intimidating bouncers aren't blocking the entrance to your gym. Physically, nothing is stopping you: You just don't feel like it. But as Burkeman asks, "Who says you need to wait until you 'feel like' doing something in order to start doing it?"

Think about that for a minute, because it's really important. Somewhere along the way, we've all bought into the idea—without consciously realizing it—that to be motivated and effective we need to *feel* like we want to take action. We need to be eager to do so. I really don't know why we believe this, because it is 100% nonsense. Yes, on some level you need to be committed to what you are doing—you need to want to see the project finished, or get healthier, or get an earlier start to your day. But you don't need to *feel like doing it.*

In fact, as Burkeman points out, many of the most prolific artists, writers, and innovators have become successful in part because of their reliance on work routines that forced them to put in a certain number of hours a day, no matter how uninspired (or, in many instances, hung over) they might have felt. Burkeman reminds us of renowned artist Chuck Close's observation that "Inspiration is for amateurs. The rest of us just show up and get to work."

So if you're sitting there, putting something off because you don't feel like doing it, remember that you don't actually *need* to feel like it. There is nothing stopping you.

Reason #3: You are putting something off because it's hard, boring, or otherwise unpleasant

Solution: Use if-then planning

Too often, we try to solve this particular problem with sheer will: *Next time, I will* make *myself start working on this sooner.* Of course, if we actually had the willpower to do that, we would never put it off in the first place. Studies show that people routinely overestimate their capacity for self-control and rely on it too often to keep them out of hot water.

Do yourself a favor and embrace the fact that your willpower is limited. Your will may not always be up to the challenge of getting you to do things you find difficult, tedious, or otherwise awful. Instead, use **if-then planning** to get the job done.

Making an if-then plan is more than just deciding what specific steps you need to take to complete a project: It's also deciding where and when you will take those steps. For example:

> *If it is 2 p.m., **then** I will stop what I'm doing and start work on the report Bob asked for. **If** my boss doesn't mention my request for a raise at our meeting, **then** I will bring it up again before the meeting ends.*

By deciding in advance *exactly* what you're going to do—and when and where you're going to do it—there's no deliberating when the time comes. There's no *Do I really have to do this now?* Or *Can this wait till later?* Or *Maybe I should do something else instead.* It's when we deliberate that willpower becomes necessary to make the tough choice. If-then plans dramatically reduce the demands placed on your willpower by ensuring that you've made the right decision way ahead of the critical moment. In fact, if-then planning has been shown in more than 200 studies to increase rates of goal attainment and productivity by 200% to 300% on average.

I realize that the three strategies I'm offering you—thinking about the consequences of failure, ignoring your feelings, and engaging in detailed planning—don't sound as fun as advice like "Follow your passion!" or "Stay positive!" But they have the decided advantage of actually being *effective*—which, as it happens, is exactly what you'll be if you use them.

HEIDI GRANT is a senior scientist at the NeuroLeadership Institute and the associate director for the Motivation Science Center at Columbia University. She is the author of *Nine Things Successful People Do Differently*, *No One Understands You and What to Do About It*, and *Reinforcements: How to Get People to Help You*. Follow her on Twitter @heidgrantphd.

Reprinted from hbr.org, originally published February 14, 2014 (product #H00OF8).

6

Productivity Tips for People Who Hate Productivity Tips

By Monique Valcour

Traditional approaches to staying focused don't work for me." "I know what I should do to be more productive, but I just don't do it." I hear sentences like these repeatedly from coaching clients. Many have read articles and books—and have even been trained in productivity methods—but still find staying focused to be an uphill battle. Why do people who know a lot about what helps people focus still struggle to focus? Through my work, I've identified several reasons, as well as strategies that may help you gain control.

Assuming that others' preferred productivity strategies should work for you can yield frustration and a sense of defeat. A friend or an author may advocate their own approach so enthusiastically that it seems foolproof if properly implemented. But if you experience the approach as inauthentic or constraining, it may not be right for you. Trying to make it work can send you into a rut where you repeat unhelpful behaviors while beating yourself up over your lack of focus.

For example, a subset of my coaching clients has an aversion to structuring their time usage with widely recommended tools like spreadsheets, planners, calendars, if-then rules, and timers. These are often the same clients who are closely attuned to the quality of their work experience, who find joy in flow and seek to create more of it, and for whom the introduction of industrial productivity levers feels stifling. If this describes you, you'll benefit by paying attention to what's happening within yourself as you work and using what you observe to inform your strategies.

If you feel defeated, two things will help you move forward and feel more in control. The first is to accept where you are and have compassion for yourself. When you admit to yourself, "I'm stuck. This feels awful," and let that admission sit in your awareness without fighting it or using it to berate yourself, it loses its power to derail you. Treat yourself with compassion by recognizing your strengths, recalling challenges you've overcome in the past, and affirming your capacity to solve problems.

Then move forward by experimenting and reflecting. I encourage my clients to check in with how their work process feels at different points throughout the day and make adjustments to improve the quality of their work experience. Being flexible helps. If one approach isn't working, try another rather than continuing to hammer away fruitlessly. Frustrated sitting at your desk? Take your work outside or to a coffee shop for a couple of hours. Computer screen making your eyes go buggy? Switch to working on paper or using voice recognition. Perhaps you're determined to complete something before lunch. But if frustration is building, stepping away, taking a walk, and getting something to eat may be exactly what you need to facilitate smooth and rapid completion of the task after lunch.

Leveraging the connection between mind and body is key to knowing when to make a change. For instance, I've learned that I need to get out of my chair to stretch several times a day. Tightness in my shoulders or numbness in my buttocks triggers the urge to move. If I feel myself hunching or my jaw getting tight, I'll walk to the window or go outside and breathe for few minutes. I also build in exercise nearly every day, typically toward the end of the workday or before something that doesn't require close attention as I find that it diffuses rather than sharpens my focus. Your body can provide you with important cues to optimally manage your focus.

Some people like to keep track of what they plan to accomplish by when. On the other hand, focusing on the process of work rather than the output is a powerfully facilitative perspective shift for many. For instance, my client Nora learned that if she framed her main goal for the day as "finish project," she felt increasingly stressed as time went by if the project wasn't moving along as quickly as she'd hoped—and she was ultimately demoralized at the end of the day if the project remained incomplete. She found she's much better served by an intention to "work on project" or "make progress on project," particularly when she identifies discrete tasks and little milestones that can serve as indicators of progress.

Staying focused doesn't have to be a struggle. While it may not be easy, managing your focus can and should be self-affirming and fulfilling. Making progress on work that is meaningful is among the most energizing and satisfying experiences anyone can have.

Therefore, it makes sense to engineer your workflow for ease and progress. University of Minnesota professor Theresa Glomb recommends organizing your work for a "downhill start."[1] Like parking your car on a slope facing downhill, what can you do to set conditions such that you need only lift your foot from the brake to get moving? Clear off your desk before you start a new task? Write down your two top priorities for the next day before leaving in the evening? Perhaps you're a big-picture person who gets bogged down in details. To move your big idea toward realization, you must pinch a manageable task out of your vision and perform it. Ask yourself, "What's one tiny step I could take?" For example, if I get an idea for an article I'd like to write, I know that the inspiration will dissipate if I don't convert it to action. I can do a rough outline in a few minutes (tangible progress). If I have time, I'll develop it into a more extensive outline (more progress). Outlining is much faster and easier than writing a whole draft, yet it's a concrete step forward that feels good and facilitates the next phase of writing. Waiting for inspiration to create something big from scratch doesn't work; in fact, it slams the brakes on productivity. What does work is finding ways to take small steps and enjoying the resulting sense of progress.

If someone else's productivity strategy feels artificial to you, it probably won't motivate you. For instance, some people can increase their productivity by setting a series of deadlines for themselves. For others, a deadline only promotes focus when it's real, interpersonally relevant, and has serious consequences attached, not when it's made up by themselves or someone else for seemingly arbitrary reasons. A real deadline for me is, for example, knowing there will be an audience waiting to hear me speak at a particular time. With that kind of deadline, I'll be ready and I will deliver an excellent talk. By contrast, me stating to myself or someone else that I plan to have my slides done two weeks in advance won't help me focus.

Productivity strategies also lose their potential to motivate when they don't feel meaningful. Try reframing something you have to do in terms of your core values for stronger and more sustained focus. Let's say I need to schedule interviews with employees at a client firm. Managing the emails and the scheduling process feels tedious if I consider these tasks mindless administrative details. But when I think of them as opening conversations that hold the key to helping people grow and thrive, they become engaging.

Many people fall prey to distractions, both internal and external, in their quest to focus. A useful tool to fend off distraction is an inquiry into the costs of giving in to it. Surrendering to distraction, while temporarily soothing, will later generate feelings of regret and even incompetence. On the other hand, making progress boosts the wonderfully self-affirming sense of mastery. In the face of temptation to give in to distraction, ask yourself the following question: "What are you saying no to right now?" When you take stock of the fact that tumbling down an internet rabbit hole means letting go of the reins and giving up time for the things you really want to do, you may well find the strength to focus.

Finally, accept that focus is dynamic, a work in progress. There's no single tool that will help you develop laser-like focus that never wanders. The best response to a few hours given over to distraction is not self-recrimination but self-compassion paired with curiosity. Regardless of whether your focus has been ideal or not, take a few moments at the end of each day to note what you accomplished and to set yourself up for a smooth downhill start on the next day's targets for progress.

MONIQUE VALCOUR is an executive coach, keynote speaker, and management professor. You can follow her on Twitter @moniquevalcour.

Note

1. Theresa Glomb, "Let's Make Work Better," filmed July 21, 2015 in Minneapolis, Minnesota, TedX Talks video, 18:35, https://www.youtube.com/watch?v=oCYeEt94EMc.

Reprinted from hbr.org, originally published December 6, 2017 (product #H03XEH).

7

5 Ways to Focus Your Energy During a Work Crunch

By Amy Jen Su

Work invariably ebbs and flows, cycling between steady states, where we feel more in control of the pace and workload, and peak periods, where the work crunch hits us hard. Unexpected setbacks, project sprints, or even vacations and holidays can create mayhem and tension. Maintaining focus and managing energy levels become critical as tasks pile onto an already full load. When you're in your next work crunch, there are a few things you can do to focus and manage your energy more productively.

Accept the situation

When an acute period hits, it's easy to resist the fact that it's happening. We wish for things to be like they were last month, or we long for the pace we had during vacation. By not being present to the here and now, we drain our energy by ruminating on the situation. In fact, physicists define resistance as "the degree to which a substance or device opposes the passage of an electrical current, causing energy dissipation." In the case of a work crunch, the more you oppose what's happening, the more energy you'll lose. Acceptance does not mean giving in.[1] On the contrary, it means acknowledging the reality of the situation with awareness so that you can take clear action.

Observe and label your underlying emotions

Acceptance is particularly difficult given the underlying emotions that an acute work crunch can bring. Negative thoughts such as *I'm not going to do a good job, I don't know if I'll be able to get it all done*, or *I feel like I'm dropping the ball at both home and work* often predominate. David Rock, director of the Neuro-Leadership Institute, suggests in his book *Your Brain at Work* that rather than suppressing or denying an emotion, an effective cognitive technique is labeling, whereby you take a situation and put a label on your emotions.[2] "The most successful executives have developed an ability to be in a state of high limbic system arousal and still remain calm," Rock says. "Partly, this is their ability to label emotion states."

The next time you are in a tough work crunch or you're experiencing a setback at work, take Rock's advice to step back, observe your thinking and emotional state, and assign a word to what's happening, such as "pressure," "guilt," or "worry." By using just one or two words, Rock's research shows, you can reduce the arousal of the limbic brain's fight-or-flight system and instead activate the prefrontal cortex, which is responsible for our executive functioning skills.

Preserve your sense of choice and agency

Accepting the situation and labeling our emotions can help reduce the anxiety that comes with a work crunch. This is critical, because, as research out of the University of Pittsburgh shows, anxiety directly impacts our cognitive functioning, especially areas that are responsible for making sound decisions.[3] Don't fall into a victim mentality, in which you believe that there are no choices or that you don't have control.

Instead, bring greater vigilance to assessing your priorities, making tough trade-offs, and incorporating self-care where you can. For example, ask yourself:

- What are the one or two things that are mission critical today?

- What is something I can do to recharge my batteries (get to bed early one night this week, listen to my favorite music while working, or catch a nap on a plane)?

- Who or what will I have to say no to during this time?

Communicate with your colleagues and loved ones

People can be a real energy drain—or gain—during work crunches and setbacks. Pause and consider how you can renegotiate deadlines, set tighter boundaries, or ask for more support during this time. Here are some suggestions.

- *Renegotiate deadlines.* Loop back with colleagues to ensure that you understand when someone really needs something and is going to review it. In other cases, if you anticipate not being able to meet a deadline, be sure to inform your colleagues of the new timing, or renegotiate it. Keep your integrity by doing what you say you're going to do and by being up front when you need to shift gears.

- *Set tighter boundaries.* Our boundaries and guardrails need to change during work crunches or acute periods. Let others in your life, both professionally and personally, know when you'll be available or not, so they will be aware of your more-limited schedule.

- *Ask for help and support.* Many of us pride ourselves on not bothering others and being self-reliant. These are great qualities, but there are times when we need to ask for help. In such times, ask your loved ones for more help on the home front. Share the weight of the accountability for projects with your colleagues by delegating or teaming up, instead of trying to do it all on your own.

Practice self-compassion

Probably the toughest thing of all during a work crunch or setback is how easy it is to beat yourself up—especially when you aren't hitting your own high standards for work or time at home. Annie McKee, author of the book *How to Be Happy at Work* and coauthor of several books on emotional intelligence, says this about self-compassion: "If you really want to deal with stress, you've got to stop trying to be a hero and start caring for and about yourself."[4]

To be truly self-compassionate, especially during an acute period of work stress, accept the situation by acknowledging it with awareness and compassion, observe and label your emotions (don't suppress or deny them), preserve your sense of choice and agency, communicate with your colleagues and loved ones, and ask for help when you need it. By taking these actions, you'll move through your next crunch with greater ease and peace.

AMY JEN SU is a cofounder and managing partner of Paravis Partners, a boutique executive coaching and leadership development firm. She is a coauthor, with Muriel Maignan Wilkins, of *Own the Room: Discover Your Signature Voice to Master Your Leadership Presence* (Harvard Business Review Press, 2013). Follow Amy on twitter @amyjensu.

Notes

1. Steve Taylor, "How Acceptance Can Transform Your Life," *Psychology Today* blog, August 19, 2015, https://www.psychologytoday.com/us/blog/out-the-darkness/201508/how-acceptance-can-transform-your-life.

2. David Rock, *Your Brain at Work: Strategies for Overcoming Distraction, Regaining Focus, and Working Smarter All Day* (New York: HarperBusiness, 2009).
3. Christopher Bergland, "How Does Anxiety Short Circuit the Decision-Making Process?" *Psychology Today* blog, March 17, 2016, https://www.psychologytoday.com/us/blog/the-athletes-way/201603/how-does-anxiety-short-circuit-the-decision-making-process.
4. Annie McKee and Kandi Wiens, "Prevent Burnout by Making Compassion a Habit," hbr.org, May 11, 2017, https://hbr.org/2017/05/prevent-burnout-by-making-compassion-a-habit.

Reprinted from hbr.org, originally published
September 22, 2017 (product #H03WMD).

8

Your Team's Time Management Problem Might Be a Focus Problem

By Maura Thomas

M y team has a time management problem," leaders often tell me. Executives might say, for example, that their teams aren't moving the needle on important projects, yet staffers seem busy and stressed. "Time management" becomes a catchall solution to this problem, and they want to hire me to offer tips and techniques on things like prioritizing and using their calendars better.

What we soon uncover, however, is that the root of the team's problems is not managing time, but managing *attention*. And these attention management issues are due not to a skills gap on the part of the employees but to a wider cultural problem unintentionally reinforced, or at least tolerated, by senior leadership.[1]

Distraction is one of the biggest hurdles to high-quality knowledge work, costing almost $1 trillion annually.[2] The first step to addressing this problem is to treat it as a company culture issue that deserves the attention of senior executives.

In my experience, many leaders inadvertently allow or even actively promote the following four situations that impede their team's ability to focus and produce their best work.

They create an environment that undermines focus

The products of knowledge work are creativity, ideas, decisions, information, and communication. All of these require extended periods of sustained focus. However, many offices have a culture in which all communication, regardless of the subject or source, carries the same level of presumed urgency and is expected to produce an immediate response.

Sometimes this happens out of a customer service requirement: Leadership mandates that customers or clients should receive timely responses to all communication. But if "timely" isn't specific and realistic, the assumption grows that faster is better—and immediate is best. Since workers never know whether incoming messages are from customers or from someone else, they must monitor messages constantly. Therefore every *other* task is tackled intermittently, in increments of 30 to 120 seconds, around the handling of messages.

Saying, "Just acknowledge the message, and let them know you'll get back to them soon" does not alleviate the problem, since workers still have to monitor their messages to know that this response is required. The problem is exacerbated when employees are issued a second computer monitor, which they use to have their email open on one screen while keeping whatever work they are trying to get done up on the other screen. This is a recipe for constant distraction, seemingly endorsed by the leaders who provide the hardware.

To solve this problem, divert customer- or client-facing issues to dedicated customer service personnel, whose role is more geared toward reactive tasks. Free up high-impact employees to have more uninterrupted time to focus on their responsibilities. If you can't designate employees for specific customer response roles, then create a realistic response window, such as four hours or one business day, perhaps with an auto-responder instructing clients to call when a timely response is required. Will your customers really leave you if you don't respond to their emails immediately? When considering customer response times, think of it this way: If your customer were sitting across from one of your employees, you wouldn't want the employee checking email. So even when the customer isn't present, the work your company provides to them deserves the same amount of respect and undivided attention, correct? If so, then your team has to have time away from incoming communication. And an added benefit is that, as studies show, that work will get done faster and better.[3]

They don't offer clear instruction on which communication channel is appropriate in which situation

Email was not designed for urgent or time-sensitive communication. Instant messaging can be a better vehicle, but it is used for trivial issues, critical issues, and everything in between. When every communication tool is used in every circumstance, there's no way to vet incoming communication except to check everything as it arrives. This ensures constant distraction.

Consider using an auto-responder or a line in your email signature that tells customers how to reach you if the matter is urgent. Also ensure that internal communication doesn't carry an expectation of immediate response. Staff, especially millennials, increasingly tend to avoid the phone and in-person communication, yet sensitive information and urgent information are better suited to these channels. Offer guidelines that are flexible yet specific regarding how to make effective use of all company communication channels.

They assign the same workers to receive and solve customer issues

Even if you designate specific staff to be the front line to customers, you will have a problem if those staff members have to both *receive* the problems and *solve* them. After all, they won't be able to bring their full attention to solving the problem if they can't take a break from receiving more problems.

Try organizing your support staff's daily schedule so that each person has time away from phone and email to thoughtfully address problems and get other meaningful work done. Another option would be to appoint a "triage" person, who only handles intake and assigns problems to others for solutions. Either choice gives support staff opportunities to devote their full attention to solving problems. This will likely result in happier customers. When staff members have a chance to reflect on issues, they are better primed to recognize systemic problems and opportunities for product and policy improvements. Train your staff to understand that good customer service means not only responding to customers in a timely manner but also solving their problems in a thorough, attentive, and satisfactory way.

They don't realize that monitoring internal systems is still work, even if there is rarely an emergency

I have this experience in almost every training session I deliver: I introduce the idea that downtime and vacation are critical for knowledge workers' success, and then the head of IT or another system-monitoring department speaks up and says that they can never be out of touch in case of a system failure. This is followed by a member of leadership jumping in to say, "But it's okay, because those kinds of emergencies rarely happen."

It's *not* okay, because monitoring work for emergencies is still *work*. If you have a staffer who is expected to be available 24/7/365 in case of an "emergency," then that person essentially gets *no* time off, because they still have to monitor their work communication "just in case." Even if there is no emergency, there's still other work happening that this staffer will see. Even if they choose not to respond, their mind will be engaged in work all the time, and there will never be a time when they can truly unplug.

To address this, every role in your organization needs to have a trusted backup. When an employee has no backup, there is risk to the business whether that employee stays or leaves. If they leave and take all of that business knowledge with them, it could take your company years to recover. If they stay, they are likely to experience high stress (which is not good for their output) or burnout (causing you to need to replace them anyway, temporarily or permanently).[4]

If you are a leader and think your employees might be struggling with "time management," examine these issues first. Your first step may be to address your culture problem around attention management. While many employees do struggle with time and attention management, the solutions won't stick unless leaders address the underlying culture issues.

MAURA THOMAS is an international speaker and trainer on individual and corporate productivity, attention management, and work-life balance. She is a TEDx speaker, was named one of *Inc.* Magazine's Top Leadership Speakers for 2018, and is the author of *Personal Productivity Secrets* and *Work Without Walls.* Follow her on Twitter @mnthomas.

Reprinted from hbr.org, originally published
February 27, 2017 (product #H03H6V).

Notes

1. Maura Thomas, "Time Management Training Doesn't Work," hbr.org, April 22, 2015, https://hbr.org/2015/04/time-management-training-doesnt-work.
2. Larry Rosen and Alexandra Samuel, "Conquering Digital Distraction," *Harvard Business Review*, June 2015, 110.
3. Peter Bregman, "How (and Why) to Stop Multitasking," hbr.org, May 20, 2010, https://hbr.org/2010/05/how-and-why-to-stop-multitaski.html.
4. Diane Coutu, "The Science of Thinking Smarter," *Harvard Business Review*, May 2008, 51.

9

How to Practice Mindfulness Throughout Your Work Day

By Rasmus Hougaard and Jacqueline Carter

You probably know the feeling all too well: You arrive at the office with a clear plan for the day, and then, in what feels like just a moment, you find yourself on your way back home. Nine or ten hours have passed but you've accomplished only a few of your priorities. And, most likely, you can't even remember exactly what you did all day. If this sounds familiar, don't worry: You're not alone. Research shows that people spend nearly 47% of their waking hours thinking about something other than what they're doing.[1] In other words, many of us operate on autopilot.

Add to this that we have entered what many people are calling the "attention economy." In the attention economy, the ability to maintain focus and concentration is every bit as important as technical or management skills. And because leaders must be able to absorb and synthesize a growing flood of information in order to make good decisions, they're hit particularly hard by this emerging trend.

The good news is you can train your brain to focus better by incorporating mindfulness exercises throughout your day. Based on our experience with thousands of leaders in more than 250 organizations, here are some guidelines for becoming a more focused and mindful leader.

First, start off your day right. Researchers have found that we release the most stress hormones within minutes after waking.[2] Why? Because thinking of the day ahead triggers our fight-or-flight instinct and releases cortisol into our blood. Instead, try this: When you wake up, spend two minutes in your bed simply noticing your breath. As thoughts about the day pop into your mind, let them go and return to your breath.

Next, when you get to the office, take 10 minutes at your desk or in your car to boost your brain with the following short mindfulness practice before you dive into activity. Close your eyes, relax, and sit upright. Place your full focus on your breath. Simply maintain an ongoing flow of attention on the experience of your breathing: Inhale, exhale; inhale, exhale. To help your focus stay on your breathing, count silently at each exhalation. Any time you find your mind distracted, simply release the distraction by returning your focus to your breath. Most important, allow yourself to enjoy these minutes. Throughout the rest of the day, other people and competing urgencies will fight for your attention. But for these 10 minutes, your attention is all your own.

Once you finish this practice and get ready to start working, mindfulness can help increase your effectiveness. Two skills define a mindful mind: *focus* and *awareness*. Focus is the ability to concentrate on what you're doing in the moment, while awareness is the ability to recognize and release unnecessary distractions as they arise. Understand that mindfulness is not just a sedentary practice; it is about developing a sharp, clear mind. And mindfulness in action is a great alternative to the illusory practice of multitasking. Mindful working means applying focus and awareness to everything you do from the moment you enter the office. Focus on the task at hand, and recognize and release internal and external distractions as they arise. In this way, mindfulness helps increase effectiveness, decrease mistakes, and even enhance creativity.

To better understand the power of focus and awareness, consider an affliction that touches nearly all of us: email addiction. Emails have a way of seducing our attention and redirecting it to lower-priority tasks because completing small, quickly accomplished tasks releases dopamine, a pleasurable hormone, in our brains. This release makes us addicted to email and compromises our concentration. Instead, apply mindfulness when opening your inbox. *Focus* on what is important and maintain *awareness* of what is merely noise. To get a better start to your day, avoid checking your email first thing in the morning. Doing so will help you sidestep an onslaught of distractions and short-term problems during a time of day that holds the potential for exceptional focus and creativity.

As the day moves on and the inevitable back-to-back meetings start, mindfulness can help you lead shorter, more effective meetings. To avoid entering a meeting with a wandering mind, take two minutes to practice mindfulness, which you can do en route. Even better, let the first two minutes of the meeting be silent, allowing everybody to arrive both physically and mentally. Then, if possible, end the meeting five minutes before the hour to allow all participants a mindful transition to their next appointment.

As the day progresses and your brain starts to tire, mindfulness can help you stay sharp and avoid poor decisions. After lunch, set a timer on your phone to ring every hour. When the timer rings, cease your current activity and do one minute of mindfulness practice. These mindful performance breaks will help keep you from resorting to autopilot and lapsing into action addiction.

Finally, as the day comes to an end and you start your commute home, apply mindfulness. For at least 10 minutes of the commute, turn off your phone, shut off the radio, and simply be. Let go of any thoughts that arise. Attend to your breath. Doing so will allow you to let go of the stresses of the day so you can return home and be fully present with your family.

Mindfulness is not about living life in slow motion. It's about enhancing focus and awareness both in work and in life. It's about stripping away distractions and staying on track with both individual and organizational, goals. Take control of your own mindfulness: Test these tips for 14 days, and see what they do for you.

RASMUS HOUGAARD is the founder and managing director of Potential Project, a global leadership and organizational development. **JACQUELINE CARTER** is a partner and the North American director of Potential Project. They are the coauthors of *One Second Ahead: Enhancing Performance at Work with Mindfulness* and *The Mind of the Leader: How to Lead Yourself, Your People, and Your Organization for Extraordinary Results* (Harvard Business Review Press, 2018).

Notes

1. S. Bradt, "Wandering Mind Not a Happy Mind," *Harvard Gazette*, November 11, 2010.
2. J. C. Pruessner et al., "Free Cortisol Levels After Awakening: A Reliable Biological Marker for the Assessment of Adrenocortical Activity," *Life Sciences* 61, no. 26 (November 1997): 2539–2549.

Adapted from content posted on hbr.org on
March 4, 2016 (#H02OTU).

10

Your Brain Can Only Take So Much Focus

By Srini Pillay

The ability to focus is an important driver of excellence. Focused techniques such as to-do lists, timetables, and calendar reminders all help people stay on task. Few would argue with that, and even if they did, there is evidence to support the idea that resisting distraction and staying present have benefits. Practicing mindfulness for 10 minutes a day, for example, can enhance leadership effectiveness by helping you become more able to regulate your emotions and make sense of past experiences.[1] Yet as helpful as focus can be, there's also a downside to focus as it is commonly viewed.

The problem is that excessive focus exhausts the focus circuits in your brain. It can drain your energy and make you lose control.[2] This energy drain can also make you more impulsive and less helpful.[3] As a result, decisions are poorly thought out, and you become less collaborative.

So what do we do then? Focus or unfocus?

Recent research shows that both focus *and* unfocus are vital. The brain operates optimally when it toggles between focus and unfocus, allowing us to develop resilience, enhance creativity, and make better decisions.[4]

When you unfocus, you engage a brain circuit called the "default mode network" (DMN). We used to think of this circuit as the "do mostly nothing" circuit because it only came on when you stopped focusing with effort. Yet when "at rest," this circuit uses 20% of the body's energy (compared with the comparatively small 5% that any effort would require).[5]

The DMN needs this energy because it is doing anything *but* resting. Under the brain's conscious radar, it activates old memories; goes back and forth between the past, present, and future; and recombines different ideas.[6] Using this new and previously inaccessible data, you develop enhanced self-awareness and a sense of personal relevance.[7] And you can imagine creative solutions or predict what might happen in the future, thereby leading to better decision-making too.[8] The DMN also helps you tune in to other people's thinking, thereby improving team understanding and cohesion.[9]

There are many simple and effective ways to activate this circuit in the course of a day. Here are some examples.

Using positive constructive daydreaming (PCD)

Positive constructive daydreaming (PCD) is a type of mind wandering that is different from slipping into a daydream or guiltily rehashing worries.[10] When you build PCD into your day deliberately, it can boost your creativity, strengthen your leadership ability, and also reenergize the brain. To activate PCD, you choose a low-key activity such as knitting, gardening, or casual reading, then wander into the recesses of your mind.[11] But unlike slipping into a daydream or guilty-dysphoric daydreaming, you might first imagine something playful and wishful—like running through the woods, or lying on a yacht. Then you swivel your attention from the external world to the internal space of your mind with this image in mind while still doing the low-key activity.

Studied for decades by psychologist Jerome Singer, PCD activates the DMN and metaphorically changes the silverware that your brain uses to find information.[12] While focused attention is like a fork that picks up obvious conscious thoughts that you have, PCD commissions a different set of silverware: a spoon for scooping up the delicious mélange of flavors of your identity (the scent of your grandmother, the feeling of satisfaction with the first bite of apple pie on a crisp fall day), chopsticks for connecting ideas across your brain (to enhance innovation), and a marrow spoon for getting into the nooks and crannies of your brain to pick up long-lost memories that are a vital part of your identity.[13] In this state, your sense of self is enhanced—which, according to organizational consultant Warren Bennis, is the essence of leadership.[14] I call this the psychological center of gravity, a grounding mechanism (part of your mental "six-pack") that helps you enhance your agility and manage change more effectively.[15]

Taking a nap

In addition to building in time for PCD, leaders can also consider authorized napping. Not all naps are the same. When your brain is in a slump, your clarity and creativity are compromised. After a 10-minute nap, studies show, you become much clearer and more alert.[16] But if it's a creative task you have in front of you, you will likely need a full 90 minutes of sleep for more complete brain refreshing.[17] Your brain requires this longer time to make more associations and dredge up ideas that reside in the nooks and crannies of your memory network.

Pretending to be someone else

When you're stuck in a creative process, unfocus can come to the rescue if you embody and live out an entirely different personality. In 2016, educational psychologists Denis Dumas and Kevin Dunbar found that people who try to solve creative problems are more successful if they behave like an eccentric poet than a rigid librarian.[18] Given a test in which they had to come up with as many uses as possible for any object (such as a brick), those who behaved like eccentric poets had superior creative performance. This finding holds even if the same person takes on a different identity.

When you're in a creative deadlock, try embodying a different identity. It will likely get you out of your own head and allow you to think from another person's perspective. (I call this "psychological halloweenism.")[19]

For years, focus has been the venerated ability amongst all abilities. Since we spend 46.9% of our days with our minds wandering away from a task at hand, we crave the ability to keep it fixed and on task.[20] Yet, if we built PCD, 10- and 90-minute naps, and psychological halloweenism into our days, we would likely preserve focus for when we needed it, and use it much more efficiently too. More important, unfocus would allow us to update information in the brain, giving us access to deeper parts of ourselves and enhancing our agility, creativity, and decision-making.

SRINI PILLAY, MD, is an executive coach and CEO of Neuro-Business Group. He is also a technology innovator and entrepreneur in the health and leadership development sectors and the author of *Tinker, Dabble, Doodle, Try: Unlock the Power of the Unfocused Mind*. He is also a part-time assistant professor at Harvard Medical School and teaches in the executive education programs at Harvard Business School and Duke Corporate Education.

Notes

1. Louise Wasylkiw et al., "The Impact of Mindfulness on Leadership in a Health Care Setting: A Pilot Study," *Journal of Health Organization and Management* 29, no. 7 (2015): 893–911; Megan Reitz and Michael Chaskalson, "Mindfulness Works, But Only If You Work at It," hbr.org, November 4, 2016, https://hbr.org/2016/11/mindfulness-works-but-only-if-you-work-at-it; Rasmus Hougaard, Jacqueline Carter, and Gitte Dybkjaer, "Spending 10 Minutes a Day on Mindfulness Subtly Changes the Way You React to Everything," hbr.org, January 18, 2017, https://hbr.org/2017/01/spending-10-minutes-a-day-on-mindfulness-subtly-changes-the-way-you-react-to-everything; Christina Congleton, Britta K. Hölzel, and Sara W. Lazar, "Mindfulness Can Literally Change Your Brain," hbr.org, January 8, 2015, https://hbr.org/2015/01/mindfulness-can-literally-change-your-brain.

2. Todd F. Heatherton and Dylan D. Wagner, "Cognitive Neuroscience of Self-Regulation Failure," *Trends in Cognitive Sciences* 15, no. 3 (March 2011): 132–139.

3. Roy F. Baumeister, "Ego Depletion and Self-Regulation Failure: A Resource Model of Self-Control," *Alcoholism: Clinical and Experimental Research* 27, no. 2 (February 2003): 281–284; C. Nathan Dewall et al., "Depletion Makes the Heart Grow Less Helpful: Helping as a Function of Self-Regulatory and Genetic Relatedness," *Personality and Social Psychology Bulletin* 34, no. 12 (December 2008): 1653–1662.

4. Jinyi Long et al., "Distinct Interactions Between Fronto-Parietal and Default Mode Networks in Impaired Consciousness," *Scientific Reports* 6 (2016): 1–11.

5. Marcus E. Raichle and Deborah A. Gusnard, "Appraising the Brain's Energy Budget," *Proceedings of the National Academy of Sciences (PNAS)* 99, no. 16 (August 2002): 10237–10239.

6. Carlo Sestieri et al., "Episodic Memory Retrieval, Parietal Cortex, and the Default Mode Network: Functional and Topical Analyses," *The Journal of Neuroscience* 31, no. 12 (March 2011): 4407–4420; Ylva Østby et al., "Mental Time Travel and Default-Mode Network Functional Connectivity in the Developing Brain," *PNAS* 109, no. 42 (October 2012): 16800–16804; Roger E. Beaty et al., "Creativity and the Default Network: A Functional Connectivity Analysis of the Creative Brain at Rest," *Neuropsychologia* 64 (November 2014): 92–98.

7. Christopher G. Davey, Jesus Pujol, and Ben J. Harrison, "Mapping the Self in the Brain's Default Mode Network," *Neuroimage* 132 (May 2016): 390–397.

8. Beaty et al., "Creativity and the Default Network," 92–98; Fabiana M. Carvalho et al., "Time-Perception Network and Default Mode Network Are Associated with Temporal Prediction in a Periodic Motion Task," *Frontiers in Human Neuroscience* 10 (June 2016): 268.

9. Christopher J. Hyatt et al., "Specific Default Mode Sub-networks Support Mentalizing as Revealed Through Opposing Network Recruitment by Social and Semantic FMRI Tasks," *Human Brain Mapping* 36, no. 8 (August 2015): 3047–3063.

10. Rebecca L. McMillan, Scott Barry Kaufman, and Jerome L. Singer, "Ode to Positive Constructive Daydreaming," *Frontiers in Psychology* 4 (September 2013): 626.

11. Benjamin Baird et al., "Inspired by Distraction: Mind Wandering Facilitates Creative Incubation," *Psychological Science* 23, no. 10 (October 2013): 1117–1122.

12. Jerome L. Singer, "Researching Imaginative Play and Adult Consciousness: Implications for Daily and Literary Creativity," *Psychology of Aesthetics, Creativity, and the Arts* 3, no. 4 (2009): 190–199.

13. Jeroen J. A. van Boxtel, Naotsugu Tsuchiya, and Christof Koch, "Consciousness and Attention: On Sufficiency and Necessity," *Frontiers in Psychology* (December 2010): 217; Christopher G. Davey, Jesus Pujol, and Ben J. Harrison, "Mapping the Self in the Brain's Default Mode Network,"

Neuroimage 132 (May 2016): 390–397; Roger E. Beaty et al., "Creativity and the Default Network," 92–98; Carlo Sestieri et al., "Episodic Memory Retrieval, Parietal Cortex, and the Default Mode Network: Functional and Topical Analyses," *The Journal of Neuroscience* 31, no. 12 (March 2011): 4407–4420.

14. Adi Ignatius, "Becoming a Leader, Becoming Yourself," *Harvard Business Review*, May 2015, 10.

15. Srini Pillay, *Tinker, Dabble, Doodle, Try: Unlock the Power of the Unfocused Mind* (New York: Ballantine Books, 2017).

16. Nicole Lovato and Leon Lack, "The Effects of Napping on Cognitive Functioning," *Progress in Brain Research* 185 (2010): 155–166.

17. Denise J. Kai et al., "REM, Not Incubation, Improves Creativity by Priming Associative Networks," *PNAS* 106, no. 25 (June 2009): 10130–10134.

18. Denise Dumas and Kevin N. Dunbar, "The Creative Stereotype Effect," *PLOS One* 11, no. 2 (February 2016): e0142567.

19. Srini Pillay, *Tinker, Dabble, Doodle, Try.*

20. Matthew A. Killingsworth and Daniel T. Gilbert, "A Wandering Mind Is an Unhappy Mind," *Science* 330, no. 6006 (November 2010): 932.

Reprinted from hbr.org, originally published
May 12, 2017 (product #H03NKH).

Index

How to be human at work.

HBR's Emotional Intelligence Series features smart, essential reading on the human side of professional life from the pages of *Harvard Business Review*. Each book in the series offers uplifting stories, practical advice, and research from leading experts on how to tend to our emotional well-being at work.

Harvard Business Review Emotional Intelligence Series

Available in paperback or ebook format. The specially priced six-volume set includes:

- Mindfulness
- Resilience
- Influence and Persuasion
- Authentic Leadership
- Happiness
- Empathy

The most important management ideas all in one place.

We hope you enjoyed this book from *Harvard Business Review*. For the best ideas HBR has to offer turn to HBR's 10 Must Reads Boxed Set. From books on leadership and strategy to managing yourself and others, this 6-book collection delivers articles on the most essential business topics to help you succeed.

HBR's 10 Must Reads Series

The definitive collection of ideas and best practices on our most sought-after topics from the best minds in business.

- Change Management
- Collaboration
- Communication
- Emotional Intelligence
- Innovation
- Leadership
- Making Smart Decisions

- Managing Across Cultures
- Managing People
- Managing Yourself
- Strategic Marketing
- Strategy
- Teams
- The Essentials

hbr.org/mustreads